# Watching with Brown

by Gregory Grissom
illustrated by Mike Dammer

Scott Foresman
is an imprint of

Glenview, Illinois • Boston, Massachusetts • Mesa, Arizona
Shoreview, Minnesota • Upper Saddle River, New Jersey

Every effort has been made to secure permission and provide appropriate credit for photographic material. The publisher deeply regrets any omission and pledges to correct errors called to its attention in subsequent editions.

Unless otherwise acknowledged, all photographs are the property of Pearson.

Photo locations denoted as follows: Top (T), Center (C), Bottom (B), Left (L), Right (R), Background (Bkgd)

Illustrations by Mike Dammer

Photograph 8 © Chris Collins/Corbis

ISBN 13: 978-0-328-39338-1
ISBN 10: 0-328-39338-X



1 2 3 4 5 6 7 8 9 10 V010 17 16 15 14 13 12 11 10 09 08

Hi! My name is Brown. Can you guess why that is my name?

I live behind the house. All kinds of things go on out here. Watch with me.

Look at the squirrel!

His arms are full of nuts. I have never seen so many nuts. What makes his cheeks so round? Nuts!

Wow! He must be hungry!

Look at that ant.

What is she pulling along? It is very big. It is a huge pear!

Wow! She must be hungry!

Look at that bird.

That bird found an apple. She is flying toward her nest. Look at her eyes! Is the apple too heavy?

Wow! She must be hungry.

When I am hungry, my owner puts out food! I am a lucky dog!

Thanks for visiting. I will eat now.

# Plants and Animals Work Together

Plants and animals help each other. Plants and animals keep each other alive!

Plants help the animals. Squirrels like to eat nuts and seeds. Ants like to eat fruit and sweet things. Birds like fruit and seeds.

Animals also help the plants. Animals carry seeds around. They drop seeds all over the place. The seeds grow into plants. Animals help make sure that plants grow in lots of places!